Kansas City

Kansas City

A Downtown America Book

Susan Sturman

Dillon Press, Inc. Minneapolis, MN 55415

Photographic Acknowledgments

Photos have been reproduced through the courtesy of Linda S. Ellis; Convention and Visitors Bureau of Greater Kansas City; Hallmark Cards, Inc./ Crown Center Redevelopment Corp.; Missouri Valley Special Collections, Kansas City Public Library; Vasco Martin/Unicorn Photo; Tom North/St. Patrick's Day Parade Committee; J.C. Nichols Co.; Worlds of Fun; Hunt Midwest Real Estate Division; and Don Witts/Missouri Town. Cover photo by David G. Johnston/Unicorn Photo.

Library of Congress Cataloging-in-Publication Data

Sturman, Susan.
   Kansas City / Susan Sturman.
     p. cm. — (A Downtown America book)
   Summary: Describes the past and present, neighborhoods, attractions, festivals, people, foods, lifestyle, historic sites, industry, and climate of Kansas City, Missouri.
   ISBN 0-87518-432-4 (lib. bdg): $12.95
   1. Kansas City (Mo.)—Juvenile literature. [1. Kansas City (Mo.)] I. Title. II. Series.
F474.K24S78 1990
977.8'411—dc20
                                   89-25614
                                      CIP
                                      AC

Dillon Press, Inc., 242 Portland Avenue South
Minneapolis, Minnesota 55415

Printed in the United States of America
1 2 3 4 5 6 7 8 9 10 99 98 97 96 95 94 93 92 91 90

About the Author

A long-time resident of the Kansas City area, Susan Sturman enjoys writing about the riverfront city. Her position as a legal assistant in a Kansas City law firm keeps her familiar with the city's rapid changes. As a freelance writer, she has published articles in a number of periodicals for both children and adults.

Contents

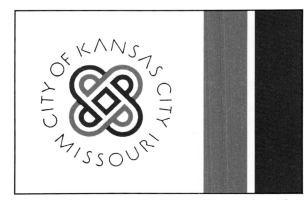

City Flag.

City Seal.

Fast Facts about Kansas City

Kansas City: City of Fountains; the River City; Crossroads of America

Location: On the western border of Missouri, about two-thirds of the way north of the corner of the state; 250 miles (400 kilometers) from the center of the United States

Area: City, 316 square miles (8,216 square kilometers); metropolitan area, 5,026 square miles (13,067 square kilometers)

Population (1990 estimate*): City, 448,159; metropolitan area, 1,525,000

Major Population Groups: Whites, African Americans, Hispanics

Altitude: *Highest*—1,105 feet (336 meters) above sea level; *Lowest*—722 feet (220 meters) above sea level

Climate: Average temperature is 30°F (-1°C) in January, 78.5°F (26°C) in July; average annual snowfall is 20.3 inches (51 centimeters); average annual rainfall is 35 inches (87 centimeters); the tornado season—April, May, and June—brings an average of six tornadoes to the city each year

Founding Date: 1838; city charter received in 1850

City Seal: Four double-lined, interlocking hearts in red, white, and blue; the words, "City of Kansas City, Missouri," surround the symbol in black print

City Flag: The official seal is centered on a white field with three vertical stripes in red, white, and blue

Form of Government: Council-manager; 13 council members, including the mayor, are each elected for four-year terms; the council appoints a city manager

Important Industries: Transportation, service, product distribution and storage, farm-related businesses

*Official 1990 U.S. Bureau of the Census figures available in 1991-92.

Festivals and Parades

January: Martin Luther King, Jr., Day celebration

March: St. Patrick's Day Parade

April: Easter Parade

May: Truman Week celebration

June: Hospital Hill Run; Kansas City Highland Games and Scottish Festival

July: Kansas City Rodeo

August: Ethnic Enrichment Festival; Kansas City Jazz Festival; Mexican Fiesta

September: Hispanic Heritage Week; Kansas City Renaissance Festival

November: American Royal Livestock, Horse Show & Rodeo; Country Club Plaza Christmas Lighting ceremony

For further information about festivals and parades, see agencies listed on page 56.

United States

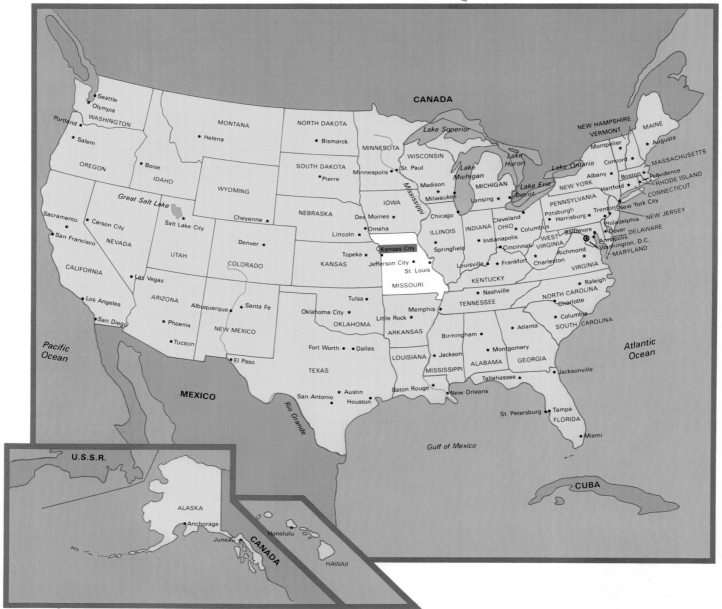

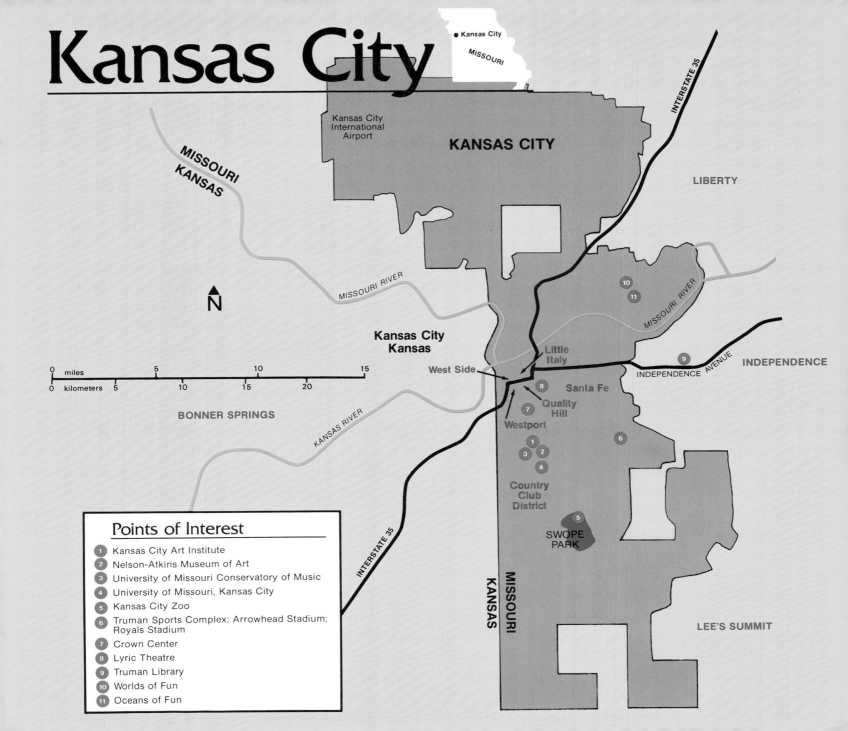

Kansas City

MISSOURI

● Kansas City

KANSAS CITY

Kansas City
International
Airport

INTERSTATE 35

LIBERTY

MISSOURI
KANSAS

MISSOURI RIVER

N

Kansas City
Kansas

Little
Italy

West Side

⑩
⑪

MISSOURI RIVER

⑨

INDEPENDENCE AVENUE

INDEPENDENCE

	miles				
0		5	10		15
0	kilometers 5	10	15	20	

BONNER SPRINGS

KANSAS RIVER

⑧ Santa Fe

⑦ Quality
Hill

Westport

①
③ ②
④

Country
Club
District

⑥

⑤

SWOPE
PARK

INTERSTATE 35

KANSAS

MISSOURI

LEE'S SUMMIT

Points of Interest

① Kansas City Art Institute
② Nelson-Atkins Museum of Art
③ University of Missouri Conservatory of Music
④ University of Missouri, Kansas City
⑤ Kansas City Zoo
⑥ Truman Sports Complex: Arrowhead Stadium;
Royals Stadium
⑦ Crown Center
⑧ Lyric Theatre
⑨ Truman Library
⑩ Worlds of Fun
⑪ Oceans of Fun

1

Going to Kansas City

Old western movies show Kansas City, Missouri, as a dusty cowtown—full of cowboys and cattle. That is an image that Kansas Citians have tried to erase. They like to call their hometown the *City of Fountains*, because more than 200 fountains rise within its boundaries. Residents also call their home the *River City*, as the Missouri River flows through the city and divides it into two sections.

Kansas City could be called the *Crossroads of America*, too. It is only 250 miles (402 kilometers) from the center of the United States, on the western border of Missouri. The Missouri River, or "Mighty Mo," winds across the city on its southeasterly course toward the Mississippi River.

North of the bluffs that border the downtown area, the Missouri River merges with the Kansas, or

The Paseo Bridge spans the Missouri River near downtown.

"Kaw," River. Across the Kaw in the state of Kansas is another Kansas City. Although it shares the same name, it is a separate city that was developed about 65 years after Kansas City, Missouri.

The original Kansas City began on the high bluffs next to the Missouri River, but has since spread across rolling hills on both sides. Smaller suburban cities such as Overland Park, Liberty, and Lee's Summit circle Kansas City to form a large metropolitan area.

There are 177 parks in Kansas City, and more miles of tree-lined boulevards than in Paris, France. Many sculptures and fountains decorate the parks. Even in the downtown business district, it is hard to find a block without a patch of green parkland.

Downtown Kansas City changed its appearance during the 1980s. Many old buildings, such as the Folly Theatre, had become rundown and were in danger of being destroyed. Although some were torn down and replaced by skyscrapers, others were restored. Amid this mix of old and new are rows of trees and flowers, and small parks where downtown workers can eat lunch or relax.

Kansas Citians come from a variety of different ethnic backgrounds. Many can trace their roots back to people who settled in the city before 1900. One out of every five residents is African American. The city is also home to smaller groups of Hispanic,

This plaza is just one of many green areas in Kansas City.

A young Kansas Citian cools off in the spray from one of the city's fountains.

Polish, Italian, and Slavic Americans. In the 1980s, many Asian people began moving to Kansas City.

One of the things people from other countries and cities notice when they move to Kansas City is the weather—it is always changing! In the winter, temperatures can reach 73°F (23°C) one day, and then drop to a chilly 9°F (-13°C) the next. In the spring, residents must be prepared for tornadoes that race through the city and surrounding areas. Once a swirling funnel cloud touches the ground, it can quickly destroy everything in its path.

Kansas City's summers are hot and sticky. The average temperature is 77°F (25°C), but can reach 100°F (38°C) or more. Relief follows on cool, crisp autumn days when the leaves turn to bright shades of red, gold, and orange.

The weather has a great effect on the agriculture-related businesses that operate in Kansas City. Farmers need enough rain and snow to produce crops such as wheat and corn. These are then stored in the city's grain elevators and used in its flour mills. Though farm-related businesses are important to Kansas City's economy, the area is home to many types of industries. Printing and publishing, food processing, and the storage and transportation of many products are all major businesses in the city.

An interesting part of the storage industry is a series of limestone caves beneath the city itself. The limestone was discovered in the nineteenth century. By mining through the layers of rock, huge caves were carved out to form underground industrial parks.

Kansas Citians are hard-working people, but they know how to balance their work with fun. The city offers many different kinds of entertainment for both visitors and residents.

Sports fans are right at home in Kansas City. In the summer, Royals Stadium is crowded with baseball fans whose cheering controls the up and down movement of a fountain. When the crowd cheers loudly, the fountain shoots water as high as 70 feet (21 meters). In the fall, local fans can choose between the Chiefs' football games at Arrowhead Stadium, or

the Comets' soccer matches in Kemper Arena.

For people who enjoy music and theater, Kansas City has plenty to offer, too. More than 40 art galleries and museums are scattered throughout the city. The Nelson-Atkins Museum of Art displays the work of famous artists such as Monet and Rembrandt. Performing arts are also popular. Some of the 12 professional theaters in Kansas City present plays just for young people.

Kansas City has its own opera, symphony, and ballet. Popular since the 1920s, jazz is still heard in some local nightclubs. This truly American music is celebrated in the annual Kansas City Jazz Festival.

Kansas City's entertainment, location, and other attractions make it an important convention center. Every fall, hundreds of blue-jacketed boys and girls come to Kansas City for the national Future Farmers of America convention. Many stay to attend the largest horse and livestock show in the country, the American Royal.

Some think it may be the food that draws more than 500 such conventions to Kansas City each year. The city boasts many fine steakhouses and several ethnic restaurants, from Italian to Vietnamese. It is probably best known for its barbecue, though.

Most people in Kansas City will proudly claim that Arthur Bryant invented barbecued food. Each day, many downtown workers take a

Arrowhead Stadium and Royals Stadium make up the Truman Sports Complex.

short drive to the inner city to visit Arthur Bryant's Barbeque. There, they find smoked meats covered with a tangy sauce. The barbecued meat is usually eaten with lard-fried potatoes. It's a tradition that Kansas Citians eagerly share with visitors.

Although Kansas City is a bustling, modern city, its traditions and history are strong. As residents watch the powerful Mighty Mo wind its way across town, many may remember that it all began with the river.

The Missouri River Queen glides toward downtown Kansas City.

2

It Started with the River

In 1820, Francis Chouteau, a French employee of the American Fur Trading Company, traveled northwest along the Missouri River from St. Louis. He was searching for a new place for his fur trading business. He found it in the wilderness where the Missouri and Kansas rivers meet. Chouteau and his bride became the first white settlers in the area in 1821.

Chouteau was more interested in trading furs than in building a city. If not for 19-year-old John Calvin McCoy, Kansas City might not have been born. In 1835, McCoy founded Westport, a trading post near the river. It offered supplies to pioneers traveling along the Santa Fe Trail. Not much more than a general store, the town gave a friendly, but rough, welcome to Kit Carson and other early scouts.

To encourage growth, McCoy

Pioneers in covered wagons such as this once traveled through Kansas City along the Santa Fe Trail.

offered free land to anyone who promised to live and work in Westport. Then in 1838, McCoy and 13 other businessmen bought 200 acres (80 hectares) along the Missouri River. The purchase included a flat rock at the river's edge that stretched four city blocks. It made a perfect boat dock. This natural levee, called Westport Landing, helped the young town become the new gateway to the West.

McCoy and the other businessmen decided the growing town needed a name. They met at the shack of One-Eyed Ellis to vote. "Possom Trot" missed by one vote, and the town was named "Town of Kansas," after a local American Indian tribe. Not until 1889 did the town get its permanent name—Kansas City.

By 1850, the Town of Kansas had several small shops, sawmills, and even a hotel. With the help of the levee, the river continued to bring new businesses to the city. Steamboats ran day and night, delivering freight to the pioneers in town.

With the growing river trade, the city's only streets—four wide gullies south of the Missouri River—could no longer handle the heavy traffic. In 1859, construction crews began cutting new streets through the high bluffs. The deep cuts left some buildings standing on 70-foot (21-meter) cliffs. One street was lowered 30 feet (9.2 meters), but residents did not move. Instead, they built onto their homes until they reached the street's new level.

A view of the excavation project in the 1860s shows the original height of the bluffs.

Many residents found this new growth exciting. Development of the city slowed in the late 1850s, however, when Kansas City became involved in the debate about slavery.

Even though Missouri was mostly a slave state, many people in the Town of Kansas did not think slavery was right. After the Civil War began in 1861, this issue destroyed the community spirit in the town. Business leaders and former friends took opposite sides of the slavery debate. All shipping trade stopped, and businesses

"The Engagement of Brush Creek," by George Burnett, details the Battle of Westport.

closed. A fourth of the population left Kansas City for safer areas. Finally, the battle of Westport was fought in October 1864. The fierce battle helped to end the Civil War in the West.

After the war, the city started to grow again. City leaders had tried to bring the railroad to town before the war began. They succeeded in 1865, and the first train rumbled through town later that year.

The transcontinental railroad helped Kansas City earn its reputa-

Floodwaters covered a large section of downtown Kansas City in 1951.

encourage whites and blacks to live in the same neighborhoods failed.

Although Kansas City covered 62 square miles (160.6 square kilometers) in 1957, most African Americans still lived in the inner city. Many wanted the same opportunities that were offered to white residents.

Some important changes occurred in the 1960s. For the first time, African Americans were elected to the city council. A law passed in 1964 required that all people be treated equally in public places such as restaurants and hotels. Slowly, the whites and blacks began sharing more and more neighborhoods and opportunities.

This racial progress was threatened after Martin Luther King, Jr., was murdered in April 1968. Riots broke out in some of Kansas City's neighborhoods. Businesses were robbed and burned. In the end, six people were killed, and many more were injured.

The riots worried both blacks and whites. Kansas Citians of all races began working harder to get along with and understand each other. Today, while there are some neighborhoods that are all black or all white, the number of peaceful, integrated neighborhoods is growing.

Kansas Citians have always tried to work together in troubled times. When two skywalks fell in the Hyatt Regency Hotel in 1981, people came from all over the city and the metropolitan area to help. Firefighters, the police, and construction workers spent almost 24 hours digging through the rubble. When they were done, they had rescued more than 200 injured people. The accident took the lives of another 114.

In 1988, a group began digging for the wreck of the steamboat *Arabia*. It had sunk just upstream from Kansas City in 1856. All 130 passengers had survived, but tons of cargo went down with the ship.

Because the river's course has changed over the years, the *Arabia*

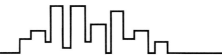

was finally uncovered in a field! The cargo included toys, flintlock rifles, beads that native Americans had used for trading, and many other items. The group that found the objects plans to display them in a river trans-port exhibit in the city.

Even with its rapid growth and big-city problems, Kansas City offers a warm, midwestern welcome. It is a place where old values of family and community are still important.

3

Living in Harmony

Each Kansas City neighborhood has its own special history and appeal. Though they may differ in backgrounds, Kansas Citians take pride in making their neighborhoods safe and beautiful places to live.

In the downtown area, the old blends with the new. Modern housing stands next to historic buildings in the Quality Hill and Union Hill neighborhoods. Both neighborhoods had become run-down, but community leaders hope new construction will attract more people to the area.

At the southern tip of downtown is Crown Center, a shopping and hotel complex. Curved walkways above the first story connect the shops to the Hyatt Regency Hotel and the Westin Crown Center Hotel. In the summertime, people gather on the outdoor terrace for free concerts.

The steeple of the Cathedral of the Immaculate Conception rises above the Quality Hill neighborhood.

Two miles (three kilometers) south of Crown Center is the oldest neighborhood in the city—Westport. Once an independent town, Westport is located along what used to be the Santa Fe Trail. A tavern, known as Boone's Store in 1850, still stands in Westport's business district. It is believed to be the oldest building in Kansas City.

The business area is filled with art galleries, shops, restaurants, and taverns. Some older two- and three-story homes have been made into apartments, which are popular with young working people.

A mansion in the southeast part of Westport houses the Nelson-Atkins Museum of Art. Within walking distance of this gallery are two cultural learning centers. The University of Missouri's Conservatory of Music and the Kansas City Art Institute attract students from other countries as well as the United States.

Each year, a festival is held in Bonner Springs, Kansas, to benefit the Art Institute. The Renaissance Festival is modeled after a medieval harvest celebration. It features jousting matches, dances, and a large variety of food.

One of the Art Institute's most famous students was Walt Disney. Disney made his first animated film in Kansas City in 1920, in a neighborhood called Santa Fe.

Located just southeast of downtown, Santa Fe was built around the turn of the century. Its multi-story

The buildings of Crown Center are connected by specially-designed curved walkways.

houses are shaded by large oak and maple trees. Before 1948, only white families were allowed to live in Santa Fe. Today, however, it is a mostly black neighborhood. Santa Fe is one of the few drug-free neighborhoods in the inner city, and the first black neighborhood in Kansas City to be listed on the National Register of Historic Places.

Not all black Kansas Citians live in neighborhoods such as Santa Fe, however. Many blacks live in low-income housing. These inner city communities have high rates of unemployment, and many young people drop out of school.

Lately, one organization has been working to fight this high drop-out rate. The Genesis Schools Writer's Project pays students to attend classes. Young people who have dropped out of school, or are planning to drop out, are paid $14 a day for five hours of class during the summer. The classes teach grammar, literature, and politics. Genesis students say the program has not only given them something to work toward, but may also help them find good jobs. As more residents find good jobs, communities will begin to improve.

To help develop the best quality of living for residents, almost all areas in Kansas City have a neighborhood association or group. One of the most active community groups is the Westside Housing Organization. It was formed to improve housing in the run-down neighborhood of West

Stately homes line some streets in Santa Fe.

Side, a few miles southwest of downtown.

In 1910, hundreds of Mexicans began to settle in West Side after fleeing from the Mexican Revolution in their homeland. Today, many of the neighborhood's residents are third-generation members of those families.

West Side families celebrate their heritage with a fiesta each year. The Mexican Fiesta is held at Our Lady of Guadalupe Church in West Side. Neighbors dress in traditional clothing and perform Mexican dances. People from all over Kansas City enjoy the food and music of the fiesta.

The Guadalupe Center helps preserve Hispanic heritage, too. Its preschool program is taught in both Spanish and English. A dance troupe sponsored by the Center teaches West Side children a variety of traditional dances. For older children, the public school system offers five Spanish "magnets."

Magnets are schools in the Kansas City, Missouri, school district that offer special courses of study along with traditional subjects. Some of the special classes are foreign languages, math and science, computer science, classical Greek, and art. The magnet program was designed to attract more students to the city's schools. A young person living in one of Kansas City's suburbs, for example, could take classes at a West Side school.

Today, West Side is home to the largest Hispanic community in the

Young Kansas Citians take part in Mexican Fiesta events.

A young leprechaun relaxes for a moment during the St. Patrick's Day parade.

metropolitan area. In 1880, though, there were so many Irish residents there that the area was called Irish Hill. It was also home to British, German, and Scandinavian immigrants.

One of the most colorful reminders of this Irish heritage is the annual St. Patrick's Day parade. Whether they can claim an Irish ancestor or not, thousands of people dress in green and fill the sidewalks along Grand Avenue on March 17. They watch marching bands, "leprechauns," and Irish clowns. Green and white floats carry hundreds of members of Irish families along the parade route.

Between the downtown business district and the south bank of the

Missouri River is River Market, one of Kansas City's older neighborhoods. Within this area are many retail shops and old warehouses that have been made into loft-style apartments and offices.

River Market began as an active steamboat landing in the 1800s. In the center of this neighborhood lies City Market. It was once a bustling town square. Since 1857, though, it has been the site of an outdoor market.

Shopping at the colorful market is a weekly event for thousands of people. Peddlers sometimes offer video games, radios, clothing, jewelry—even live ducks and rabbits.

Along the eastern edge of River Market is another early riverfront

Visitors to City Market can find everything from fruit to these furry rabbits.

Brilliant lights decorate the buildings of Country Club Plaza during the Christmas season.

neighborhood. Little Italy, or North End as it is also called, was settled in 1890 by a group of Roman Catholics who arrived from Italy. While today's neighborhood is a mix of Italians, blacks, Asians, and whites, the early Italian influence can still be seen. Older homes have long, open porches, and some homes display religious statues.

As Little Italy was being founded, a young Kansas Citian traveled to England and was impressed by the many elegant neighborhoods he saw there. Those sights caused him to build a similar community, 4 miles (6.4 kilometers) south of downtown, in 1907. The Country Club District is now an area of stately homes and curving, tree-lined streets.

Amid these homes is Loose Park, where the Battle of Westport was fought in 1864. The 74-acre (29.6-hectare) park features a duck pond, wading pool, jogging path, and a prize-winning rose garden filled with 4,000 rose bushes.

On the northern border of the Country Club District is the Country Club Plaza, built in 1923. This shopping center is one of the oldest in the country. Here, people can view the Spanish style of architecture and the European fountains from horse-drawn carriages that circle the Plaza.

With all it has to offer, the area is best known for its "Plaza lights." Forty-seven miles (75 kilometers) of Christmas lights outline the buildings during the holiday season. This beautiful display of color is just one more reason Kansas Citians take pride in their city's neighborhoods.

4

A City of Opportunity

Kansas City has a variety of businesses that provide many different jobs. If one type of business fails, there are other industries to give jobs to Kansas Citians. The city is also a leader in transportation, farm-related businesses, product distribution and storage, and service industries.

Kansas City's location is one reason businesses are drawn to the area. Shipping time and expenses are lower from Kansas City than from other U.S. cities because it is in the center of the country. Also, storage costs are less when using the area's system of limestone caves.

Long corridors in the caves allow trucks and trains to rumble through on their way to load and unload merchandise. Because the caves are underground, the temperature stays cool year-round, which is good for storing

Railroad cars are unloaded in the limestone caves beneath the city.

most items. The savings in energy costs have added to the caves' popularity.

One part of the storage space is called the foreign trade zone. It is used for international trade. Because of this, Kansas City is home to more than 40 multinational businesses. The city is also the location of the only U.S. office of the Japan Chamber of Commerce and Industry.

Foreign goods can be delivered to the trade zone and stored without paying taxes, called duties. The duty is not paid until the merchandise leaves the zone and enters United States Customs territory. Companies can save money by using the zone as factory space to inspect, test, and assemble their products before shipping.

Once a product is ready for shipping from the caves, the owner must choose a method of transport. At this point, the many transportation companies in the city take over.

Rail service is important to Kansas City today, just as it was in 1865. With 11 railroads serving the area, there are 300 trains moving in and out of the city each day. Although passenger service is offered by Amtrak, most of the city's trains are used to haul freight.

When speed is important, products and people may travel by air. More than 105,000 tons of freight are flown in and out of Kansas City International Airport (KCI) and the downtown airport each year. Trans World Airlines (TWA), which operates out

A crane loads a waiting barge on the Missouri River.

of KCI, employs more than 5,000 Kansas Citians.

A grassy hill separates the downtown airport from the city's oldest means of travel—the river. Kansas City is the largest port on the Missouri River. More than 2.5 million tons of freight are shipped in and out of Kansas City each year.

Wheat is one of the products that is often shipped by river barges. Because it is in the center of the nation's breadbasket, the Kansas City area is known as the capital of the milling and baking world.

Half of the wheat grown in the United States is called hard red winter wheat. It is farmed mostly in the Great Plains states and is used to bake bread. The Kansas City Board of Trade is the largest market for this wheat. Contracts for billions of bushels of wheat change hands on the busy trading floor each year.

Buyers and sellers work in an area called the pit. They agree on a price for the grain that will be delivered in Kansas City. The traders settle on the prices by yelling and using hand signals. Brightly colored jackets are worn to help attract attention. The prices set at the Kansas City Board of Trade set the price of wheat for the rest of the world.

Much of the wheat delivered to Kansas City is used locally. Large millers such as General Mills, ConAgra, and ADM Milling Company grind the grain into flour.

While milling provides Kansas Citians with many jobs, it is not the only agricultural business here. Large companies such as Mobay Corporation and Farmland Industries make equipment and products used by farmers. Some of Mobay's products keep farm animals healthy.

Healthy cattle and hogs are especially important to buyers and sellers at the Kansas City Stockyards. Trading dropped at the Stockyards after the 1951 flood when many meat packing companies went out of business. While the Stockyards' business has

never been the same, it is still the best place for the area's small farmers to sell their livestock.

In addition to its farm-related industries, Kansas City is also home to many banks. The city is known as a regional banking center. Yet banking is just one part of Kansas City's service industry. One well-known service company is Hallmark Cards. The greeting card firm employs more than 5,000 workers in and around Kansas City. The biggest employer in the service industry, though, is the U.S. government. More Kansas Citians work for the federal government than for any other employer.

Kansas Citians have shown that small businesses, too, can grow in their city. In fact, one local firm grew so large that it is now an internationally known company. Henry and Richard Bloch opened an office in Kansas City in the mid-1950s and began preparing tax returns. Their company, H&R Bloch, now prepares more than 13 million tax returns worldwide each year.

Since the 1880s, Kansas City has proven itself to be a city of opportunity. Although the times and needs of the people have changed, the hard-working spirit of the city remains strong.

5

Sights and Sounds of Kansas City

Kansas Citians say it is hard to get bored in their hometown. No matter what the day or season, there always seems to be something happening.

The city's cold, wintry days can be spent in many ways. Kansas Citians can take advantage of the children's theaters, museums, and Kaleidoscope, an art workshop just for children. After a heavy snowfall, residents might take their sleds and toboggans to the hilly parks around town. Winter is also a time for ice skating—indoors and outdoors— or building snow forts.

On warm days, Kansas Citians use the 20,000 acres (8,000 hectares) of parkland, 23 miles (37 kilometers) of biking trails, and dozens of free fishing lakes throughout the city. Both children and adults can take part in almost any sport through a commun-

One of the busy Kaleidoscope workshops.

Kansas Citians feed the ducks at Swope Park.

ity program in their neighborhood.

When Colonel Swope donated land for a park in 1896, people laughed at his gift. It was 4 miles (6.4 kilometers) outside the city limits. Today, Swope Park is a welcome playground of beautiful trails and forest-lined picnic grounds, almost at the center of the city. Within the park are golf courses, fishing lakes, bike trails, ball diamonds, tennis courts, and a nature center. Model airplanes soar above a field reserved for that special use. At the northwest edge of the park is the Starlight Theatre. During summer months, Broadway musicals and modern concerts are presented there in an outdoor amphitheater.

The Kansas City Zoo stretches across 80 acres (24 hectares) of Swope Park. Many animals roam in settings designed to look like the areas where they lived in the wild. In the African veldt, visitors can view Casey, a 10,000-pound (4,540-kilogram) bull elephant, believed to be the largest in the United States. Some other favorite places in the zoo are the Touchtown petting zoo, the zoo nursery, and the great cat walk.

People of all ages enjoy Worlds of Fun and Oceans of Fun. The two parks cover 225 acres (90 hectares) of land north of the Missouri River.

A resident of the Kansas City Zoo clowns for visitors.

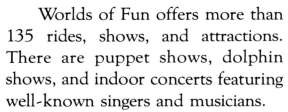

The Orient Express.

Worlds of Fun offers more than 135 rides, shows, and attractions. There are puppet shows, dolphin shows, and indoor concerts featuring well-known singers and musicians.

A favorite ride at the park is the Orient Express. This roller coaster plunges 115 feet (35 meters) and travels through two upside-down loops before coming to a stop. The Timber Wolf, Zambezi Zinger, and the EXT are also popular rides.

Relief from the summertime heat can be found on water rides such as the Viking Voyager and Fury of the Nile—or simply by walking next door to Oceans of Fun.

There are more than 35 water attractions at Oceans of Fun. Young children can play at the fountains,

wading pools, and slides in a section called Knee-Hai Belly-Hai. Adults and older children may enjoy the twisting, 900-foot (274.5-meter) water slides of Diamond Head. Or they may enjoy floating through the rushing waters of the Caribbean Cooler. There is a lake for riding paddle boats, too, as well as an old-fashioned swimming hole. One of the most popular attractions is the Surf City Wave Pool, where a million gallons of water form waves just right for body surfing and rafting.

The Missouri River offers a peaceful setting for another form of water entertainment—riverboat cruising. The Missouri River Queen is a triple-decker boat built to look like a mid-nineteenth century sternwheeler.

As passengers board the boat, music is played from a calliope, an old-fashioned instrument similar to an organ. Narrated trips allow a close-up view of the riverfront during the day. At night, passengers may choose from a variety of dinner cruises, complete with live entertainment.

Kansas City is proud of its pioneer past. The public may view the city's Old West heritage through many historic homes, sites, and museums. One interesting place to visit is Missouri Town 1855, about 19 miles (30.6 kilometers) east of downtown on the eastern side of Lake Jacomo.

Missouri Town is a collection of 25 buildings dating back to 1820. The schoolhouse, livery stable, cabins, and other buildings were discov-

A candle-dipping demonstration at Missouri Town.

ered in various parts of the area and then transported to Missouri Town.

The site is a living museum. Volunteers dressed like people from the 1850s demonstrate the daily life of settlers. Visitors can watch long-bearded men as they perform wood-working and blacksmithing tasks. In Samuel Tavern, biscuits are baked in a small iron oven atop the red-hot coals of a brick fireplace.

Special activities are presented at Missouri Town throughout the year. At Christmas, an open house features church services, a friendship tea, and caroling. Ladies in cotton prairie dresses tell stories of life in this area as it was in 1855.

More sites honoring the past are located northwest of Missouri Town in Independence. In 1945, Harry S. Truman, a Kansas City judge, became the thirty-third president of the United States. The Harry S. Truman Library and Museum contains gifts to the former president from heads of state, and many exhibits relating to his presidency.

Visitors enjoy touring a room which is decorated to look like the president's Oval Office. They can also see an 18-foot (5.5-meter)-long model of the battleship USS *Missouri*. On the wall is a copy of a 1948 edition of the *Chicago Tribune*. The headlines announced Truman's defeat in the presidential election while the votes were still being counted. As it turned out, he won.

The public may also visit a restored courtroom where Truman served as county judge. The Truman family home, built by Bess Truman's grandfather in 1862, is also in Independence.

Historic monuments are only one part of the Kansas City experience. Visitors and residents alike can enjoy the city's many theaters, relax in its quiet parks, or cruise along the Missouri River. No longer a dusty cowtown, Kansas City is a lively, exciting place to live in and visit.

Places to Visit in Kansas City

Historical Museums

Black Archives of Mid-America
2033 Vine Street
(816) 483-1300

Jesse James Bank Museum
103 N. Water Street
Liberty, Missouri
(816) 781-4458

Kansas City Museum
3218 Gladstone Boulevard
(816) 483-8300

Missouri Town 1855
Fleming Park, east side of Lake Jacomo
Blue Springs, Missouri
(816) 881-4431

Harry S. Truman Home
219 S. Delaware Street
Independence, Missouri
(816) 254-7199

Harry S. Truman Library & Museum
U.S. Highway 24 & Delaware Street
Independence, Missouri
(816) 833-1225

Other Museums

Nelson-Atkins Museum of Art
4525 Oak Street
(816) 561-4000

Toy & Miniature Museum
5235 Oak Street
(816) 333-2055

Theaters

Folly Theater
300 West 12th
(816) 474-4444

Lyric Theatre
11th & Central streets
(816) 471-7344
State Ballet of Missouri; the Kansas City Symphony; the Lyric Opera

Missouri Repertory Theatre
4949 Cherry Street
(816) 276-2700

Starlight Theatre
4600 Starlight Road
(816) 333-9481

Theatre for Young America
7204 W. 80th Street
(816) 648-4600

Tiffany's Attic
5028 Main Street
(816) 561-7529

Waldo Astoria
7428 Washington Street
(816) 561-7529

Special Attractions

Arrowhead Stadium
1 Arrowhead Drive
(816) 924-3333
Kansas City Chiefs

City Market
5th & Walnut streets
(816) 274-1341

Kaleidoscope
25th Street at McGee Street
(816) 274-8300

Kansas City Zoo
6700 Zoo Drive
Swope Park
(816) 333-7405

Kemper Arena
1800 Genessee Street
(816) 421-7770
Kansas City Comets

Missouri River Queen
1 River Drive
Kansas City, Kansas
(913) 281-5300

Oceans of Fun
I-435, exit 54
(816) 459-9283

Royals Stadium
1 Royal Way
(816) 921-8000
Kansas City Royals

Worlds of Fun
I-435, exit 54
(816) 454-4444

Chamber of Commerce Greater Kansas City
920 Main Street
Kansas City, Missouri 64105
(816) 221-2424

Convention and Visitors Bureau of Kansas City
1100 Main Street
Kansas City, Missouri 64105
(816) 221-5242

Kansas City: A Historical Time Line

1821	Francois Chouteau settles at the junction of the Missouri and Kansas Rivers
1835	Westport is founded
1838	Town of Kansas (later known as Kansas City) is founded
1850	Town of Kansas receives a charter
1864	Last Civil War battle is fought in Kansas City area
1865	Railroad extends to Kansas City
1869	The first Hannibal Bridge opens
1870	Construction begins on Kansas City Stockyards
1896	Acquisition of the first 1,350 acres of Swope Park
1914	Union Station opens
1917	Second Hannibal Bridge opens
1922	First horse and livestock show is held in the American Royal Building
1923	Country Club Plaza opens
1939	Tom Pendergast sent to prison, ending Pendergast administration
1951	Flood destroys many homes and 5,000 head of livestock
1956	Broadway Bridge opens, replacing obsolete Hannibal Bridge
1970	The Kansas City Chiefs win the Super Bowl
1972	Arrowhead Stadium opens; Kansas City International Airport opens
1973	Royals Stadium opens
1981	Hyatt Regency Hotel skywalks collapse; 114 people killed, many more are injured
1985	The Kansas City Royals win the World Series
1988	Arson explosion kills six firefighters

Index